Contents

KT-164-733

Words that appear in **bold** can be found in the glossary on page 30.

The Science Detective, Sherlock Bones, will help you learn all about Forces and Motion. The answers to Sherlock's questions can be found on page 31.

What are forces?

The world is full of things that move. Cars travel along the road, rain falls from the sky and leaves blow in the wind. This movement happens because of forces. To make an object move, a force is needed to push or pull it.

Pushes and pulls

Forces can be large or small. They cause objects to move or change the way that things move. Forces are pushes and pulls. We move a door by pushing or pulling it open or closed. When we ride a bike, we push on the pedals and we push and pull the handlebars to steer. We usually push things away from us and pull things towards us.

▼ **When you ride a bicycle, you use lots of pushes and pulls.**

SCIENCE AT WORK

Forces can be measured. We measure them in **Newtons** (N) – named after the English scientist Sir Isaac Newton in recognition of his work investigating forces. One Newton is the downward force of 100 grams (4 oz). This is about the **weight** of an apple. Forces can be measured using an instrument called a **forcemeter** (or a newtonmeter).

Body pushes down on the seat

Hands push and pull the handlebars

Feet push the pedals

THE SCIENCE DETECTIVE INVESTIGATES

Forces and Motion

Katie Dicker

WAYLAND

First published in 2010 by Wayland

Copyright © Wayland 2010
This paperback edition published in 2011 by Wayland

Wayland
338 Euston Road
London NW1 3BH

Wayland Australia
Level 17/207 Kent Street
Sydney, NSW 2000

Produced for Wayland by
White-Thomson Publishing Ltd

www.wtpub.co.uk
+44 (0)845 362 8240

Senior editor: Camilla Lloyd
Designer: Clare Nicholas
Consultant: Jon Turney
Picture researcher: Amy Sparks
Illustrator: Stefan Chabluk
Sherlock Bones artwork: Richard Hook

British Library Cataloguing in Publication Data:
 Dicker, Katie.
   Forces and motion. — (The science detective investigates)
   1. Force and energy—Juvenile literature. 2. Motion—
   Juvenile literature. 3. Force and energy—Experiments—
   Juvenile literature. 4. Motion—Experiments—Juvenile
   literature.
   I. Title II. Series
   531.1'1-dc22

ISBN 978 0 7502 6689 5

Printed in China

Wayland is a division of Hachette Children's Books, an Hachette UK company.

www.hachette.co.uk

Picture Acknowledgments:
Abbreviations: t-top, b-bottom, l-left,
r-right, m-middle.
Cover: Istockphoto (Ben Blankenburg)
Insides: Folios Dreamstime (Seraphic);
1 Dreamstime (Garyertter); **4**
Dreamstime (Kurhan); **5** Shutterstock
(Ekaterina Starshaya); **6** Dreamstime
(Sabphoto); **7** NASA; **8** Istockphoto
(Jason Lugoh); **8-9** Photolibrary (Pete
Stone); **9** NASA; **10** Shutterstock
(Laurent Renault); **11** (t) Istockphoto
(Bojan Fatur), (b) Dreamstime (Eastwest
Imaging); **12** Istockphoto (Strickke); **13**
Photolibrary (Birgid Allig); **14** (t)
Istockphoto (Ben Blankenburg), (b)
Dreamstime (Vika12345); **15**
Photolibrary (Michael Weber); **16**
Dreamstime (r Garyertter, l Weberfoto);
18 Photolibrary (Darren DeSoi); **19**
Corbis (Moodboard); **20** Corbis (Image
Source); **22** Dreamstime (José
Marafona); **23** (t) Dreamstime
(Devonyui), Getty Images (r Dorling
Kindersley, b George Diebold); **24**
Dreamstime (Seraphic); **25** Istockphoto
(t Alan Aga, b Konstantin Petkov); **26**
Corbis (Ole Graf); **27** Dreamstime
(Olavin); **29** Dreamstime (Marcoinno).

THE SCIENCE DETECTIVE INVESTIGATES:
Pushes and pulls

Look at the following objects and think about how you would move them. Do you push or pull the object – or both?

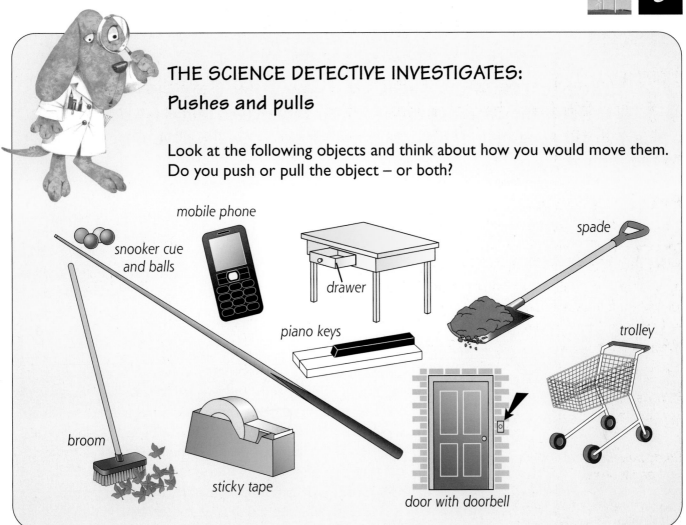

mobile phone

snooker cue and balls

drawer

piano keys

spade

trolley

broom

sticky tape

door with doorbell

Forces in nature

We use our own muscles to push or pull the objects around us, but forces are found in nature, too. The force of the wind causes trees to rustle, washing to dry and windmills to turn. The force of water causes pebbles to tumble along the bottom of a stream. We can't see forces but we can see or feel their effects. In the wind, we notice a door banging shut or an umbrella turning inside out. If you've ever banged your elbow, you'll have noticed the force as a sharp pain!

▼ **An umbrella turns inside out when it is pushed by the force of the wind.**

What is gravity?

Gravity is a force found in nature. This invisible force pulls everything towards the centre of the Earth. Gravity makes things fall downwards. If you jump up in the air, the force of gravity will pull you back down to the ground again.

Weight

The pull of gravity makes things feel heavy – it gives them weight. The more there is of something, the greater the pull of gravity and the heavier it feels. A polystyrene block is lighter than a stone brick because it is full of air bubbles. The force of gravity makes the brick feel heavier because there is lots of stone to pull towards the ground.

Gravity in space

The force of gravity works between two objects. We are pulled towards the centre of the Earth, and the Earth is pulled towards the centre of our bodies. But because the Earth is huge in comparison, it attracts us with a greater force. Objects are pulled towards the centre of the Moon, too, but because the Moon is smaller than the Earth, its gravity is weaker. The Moon is also pulled by the Earth's gravity, which is why it stays in **orbit** (moves around) the Earth. In a similar way, the Earth is attracted by the Sun's gravity and orbits the Sun.

◀ **When you jump to catch a ball, the force of gravity pulls you down again.**

▼ **Wherever you are on Earth, the force of gravity pulls you towards the Earth's centre.**

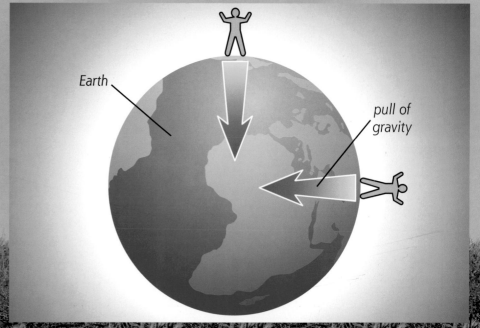

Earth

pull of gravity

▲ An astronaut weighs six times less on the Moon than on Earth because the force of gravity is weaker.

🐾 Why do you think astronauts walk on the Moon in a strange way?

SCIENCE AT WORK

The centre of gravity is the point at which something balances. Your centre of gravity can change. If you wear a heavy rucksack, you will find it more difficult to balance when you sit down because your centre of gravity has shifted towards the rucksack. In Africa, some people carry pots and baskets on their head when they collect water and food to eat. The objects balance because they are positioned over the centre of gravity.

THE SCIENCE DETECTIVE INVESTIGATES:

Clown tricks

You will need:
• ping-pong ball • scissors • sheet of A4 paper
• sticky tape • coloured pens • modelling clay

1 Ask an adult to help you cut the ping-pong ball in half. Roll the sheet of paper into a tube and put the end inside one half of the ping-pong ball. Tape the paper to the ping-pong ball, to make a curved edge at the bottom.
2 Draw a clown's face at the top of the paper tube and decorate the body. Try to stand your clown on a flat surface. You should find that it falls over.
3 Now drop a small ball of modelling clay into the base of the ping-pong ball. Try to stand the clown up. What happens this time? Now try to push the clown over. What happens?

A4 paper

ping-pong ball

What are balanced forces?

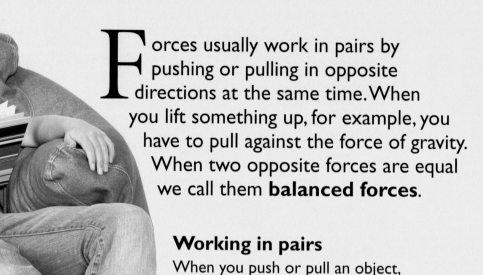

Forces usually work in pairs by pushing or pulling in opposite directions at the same time. When you lift something up, for example, you have to pull against the force of gravity. When two opposite forces are equal we call them **balanced forces**.

Working in pairs

When you push or pull an object, an opposite force tries to **resist** it. When you sit on a chair, your body pushes down on the chair but the chair pushes up against your body, too. Your body will stay still if the opposite forces are equal. If the forces become unbalanced, however, some movement will occur.

▲ You sink into a beanbag because your weight is greater than the upward force of the beanbag. As the beads move and settle, the forces become balanced and you stay in one position.

🐾 **Why is it difficult to walk on sand?**

Unbalanced forces

If you sit on a broken chair, the force of your body will be greater than the force of the chair pushing against you and you will fall to the ground. When a rocket launches, the powerful force of the engines is greater than the force of gravity pulling on the rocket, so the rocket lifts into the air. **Unbalanced forces** are used in a game of tug-of-war, too. The team with the strongest pull is able to move the rope across the line. Without unbalanced forces, things would stay in one position all the time.

SCIENCE AT WORK

When an object is already moving, balanced and unbalanced forces have a similar effect. If the forces are balanced (or there is no force), the object will keep moving at the same speed. If the forces are unbalanced, the object will speed up or slow down.

▲ Unbalanced forces help this rocket to launch into the air.

▼ In this tug-of-war competition, the team in white have the strongest pull. They have pulled the other team over the white line.

How do forces change an object's shape?

Forces change the way things move, but they can also affect an object's shape. If an unbalanced force acts on an object, it may cause it to dent or squash. The bigger the force, the more the shape is changed.

Types of movement

Forces can cause objects to move in different ways. A pull may stretch some objects, while a push can squeeze them. A push or a pull can also cause a twisting motion. More than one force can act on an object at the same time. When you chew your food, for example, your powerful jaw muscles push and pull your jawbones. This helps your teeth to squash and tear your food so it is small enough to swallow. When you work with modelling clay, you squash, stretch and twist the clay into different shapes.

Temporary or permanent?

A large force can permanently change the shape of some objects. If you hit a metal object with a hammer, the force may cause a dent in the metal's surface. This dent will be difficult to remove without another force to push the metal back again. Some objects keep their shape when a force is applied. You can stretch an elastic band, for example, but it will snap back to its original shape when you let go. We say that the band has **elasticity**. Elastic objects stretch, but if the force becomes too big they may break or snap.

▲ Modelling clay is a material that can be stretched, squashed and twisted to change its shape.

STAY SAFE

Be careful when stretching elastic bands. They can snap if you stretch them too far, or flick painfully against your skin (or other people) when you let go.

SCIENCE AT WORK

Some objects have to be heated before their shape can be changed. When a **blacksmith** shapes iron or steel, for example, the metal has to be heated in a forge (fire) to make it softer. The blacksmith hammers the hot metal to cut, bend and flatten it into shapes such as horseshoes or metal tools.

▼ This fitness ball squashes slightly when you push against it. It returns to its original shape when you let go.

🐾 Can you think of five objects that go back to their original shape when they are stretched?

How do forces change the way things move?

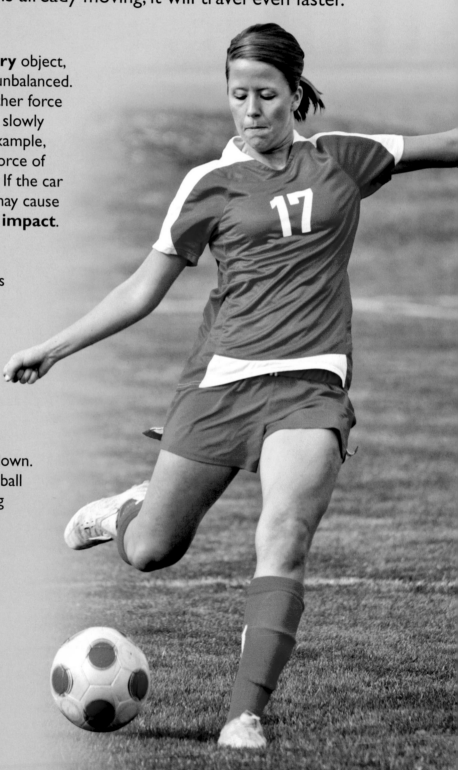

Forces cause objects to move from place to place, but they can also change the way things move. Large forces make an object move quickly. If you add a force to an object that is already moving, it will travel even faster.

Starting and stopping

When a force is applied to a **stationary** object, it will begin to move if the forces are unbalanced. The object will keep moving until another force causes it to stop. If a toy car is moving slowly along the ground and hits a wall, for example, the car will stop moving because the force of the wall acts in the opposite direction. If the car is travelling fast, the force of the wall may cause the car to move backwards slightly on **impact**.

Different directions

When an object is moving, extra forces can cause the object to **accelerate** (speed up), **decelerate** (slow down) or change direction. When you kick a football, the harder you kick the ball, the faster it moves. The increase in speed will depend on the weight of the ball and the size of the force from your foot. If a ball is travelling fast, and you kick it softly, it will begin to slow down. You can also change the direction of a ball by kicking it at a different angle. Moving objects travel in a straight line unless a force acts on them.

▶ **Kicking a ball can change its speed and direction.**

🐾 **When you ride a bicycle, what do you have to do to go faster? How do you slow down?**

◄ **Pushing someone on a swing makes them move faster. If you push in the same direction as the swing is moving, the movement will be even faster.**

THE SCIENCE DETECTIVE INVESTIGATES:

Car race

You will need:
- pile of books • long strip of stiff card • selection of toy cars and trucks (different shapes and sizes) • measuring tape • notebook and pencil

1 Make a ramp by resting one end of the card on the pile of books. Gently release each car and truck down the ramp and look at how they move. Which vehicles move the fastest? Which move the slowest? How far do they travel?

2 Remove or add books to make the ramp flatter or steeper. Measure the distance each vehicle travels (from the top of the ramp to where the vehicle stops). Compare these distances to the height of the ramp. Draw a graph to record your findings.

3 How can you make the vehicles travel further? Which cars or trucks go a long way? How would you ensure that your comparisons are fair?

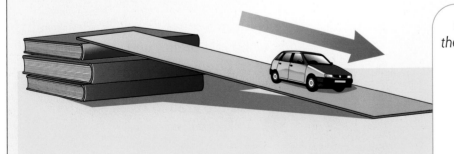

This graph shows the different distances that four vehicles travel when they move down a ramp.

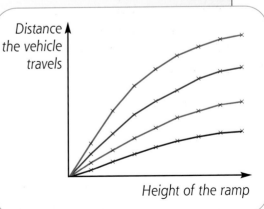

Distance the vehicle travels

Height of the ramp

What is friction?

When two objects rub together, they make a force called **friction**. Friction slows down moving objects or causes stationary objects to stay still. When you pick something up, the friction between your fingertips and the object stops it from slipping from your grasp.

Rough and smooth

There is more friction between rough surfaces than between smooth surfaces. Rough sandpaper is used to smooth a piece of wood because the friction between the two surfaces causes them to wear away. If you rubbed the wood with a smooth piece of paper or plastic, there would be very little friction to scratch the surface. Sandpaper is useful, but friction can be a nuisance, too. Friction can wear away the parts of moving machinery, which have to be replaced. A hole in the sole of your shoe can be caused by friction between your shoe and the ground. It will keep getting bigger the more that you wear it.

Slowing down

Friction slows things down because it acts in the opposite direction of a moving object. When a book slides across a table, it will slow down and eventually stop because the friction between the book and the table opposes the forward motion of the book. In contrast, skis run smoothly on snow and ice skates glide on ice, because there is very little friction to slow them down. Friction can be a nuisance but it can be useful, too. The friction between your bicycle brakes and the front wheel helps to slow you down, and the friction between the rough soles of your shoe and the ground stops you from slipping over.

▲ A snowboard has a smooth surface that reduces friction between the snow and the board.

🐾 Why does a car skid when it brakes on an icy road?

◀ The ridges on the bottom of these hiking boots give your feet a firm grip on the ground.

▼ Gymnasts cover their hands with chalk powder to absorb moisture. The chalk also reduces friction so their skin can move freely over the apparatus.

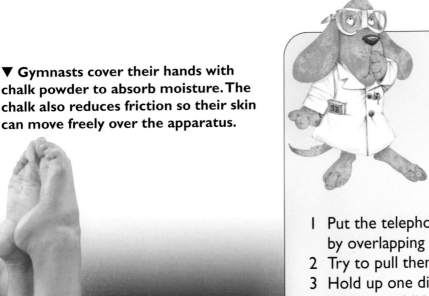

THE SCIENCE DETECTIVE INVESTIGATES:

Friction magic

You will need:
• 2 telephone directories

1 Put the telephone directories together by overlapping lots of pages.
2 Try to pull them apart. What happens?
3 Hold up one directory and try to let the other one fall. What happens?
4 Now try with just a few overlapping pages. What happens this time?

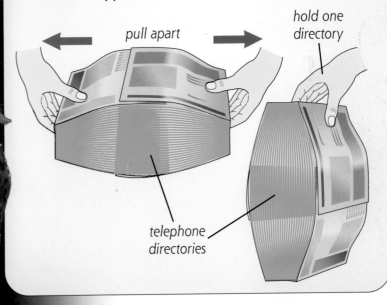

pull apart

hold one directory

telephone directories

SCIENCE AT WORK

Have you had difficulty twisting open a jam jar lid? If you wear a pair of rubber gloves, you will find it easier to open the jar. This is because the rubber creates more friction than your hands, increasing the force of your twisting motion.

What is air resistance?

Friction affects two solids rubbing together, but it can also affect objects moving through air. This type of friction is called **air resistance** (or **drag**). When air rubs against moving objects, it slows them down. We can feel air resistance when we try to walk against the wind.

Streamlined shapes

The size and shape of a surface affects how fast something moves through the air. If you stretch your arms out wide when you walk in the wind, it will be more difficult to move. This is because the air is pushing against a greater surface area. Cars, trains and planes are designed to have a **streamlined** shape. Their design helps to reduce the amount of friction so the vehicles can move smoothly through air. If friction is reduced, vehicles can move faster and use less fuel to move from place to place.

▶ **This cyclist is wearing tight clothes and a helmet that is shaped to be streamlined, to help him move faster.**

Using air resistance

Air resistance slows us down, but it can also be useful. When a skydiver falls from a plane, a parachute helps to slow the fall for a soft landing. The shape and surface area of the parachute creates air resistance that acts against the pull of gravity. The bigger the parachute, the more air is trapped and the slower the fall.

◀ **When a parachute moves through the air, its surface and shape increase the air resistance, slowing it down.**

SCIENCE AT WORK

Air resistance causes objects to fall at different speeds. In a **vacuum** there is no air resistance. If you dropped a feather and a coin from a tall building in a vacuum, they would reach the ground at the same time because the pull of gravity causes them to fall at the same speed. In air, the feather falls more slowly because air resistance works against its light weight, shape and surface as it falls.

Why do sports cars have a smooth, sleek shape?

THE SCIENCE DETECTIVE INVESTIGATES:

Falling parachutes

You will need:
- 10 paper plates • hole punch • string • scissors • 10 weighted beads
- sharp pencil • tape measure • stopwatch

1 On each paper plate (your parachute canopy), punch four holes at equal distances around the edge. Cut two lengths of string (50 cm / 20 in) for each plate. Thread them through a weighted bead, and tie each end to opposite holes. The bead will help to stabilise your parachute when it falls.
2 Ask an adult to help you punch some more holes in the paper plates, using the sharp pencil and the hole punch. In each plate, make a different number of holes of different sizes.
3 Using the measuring tape, hold a paper plate 1.5 m (5 ft) above the ground, with the string and the bead hanging down. Ask a friend to start the stopwatch when you let go, and watch your 'parachute' float to the floor. How long does each parachute take to reach the ground? How do the number and size of holes affect the speed? How will you ensure that your comparisons are fair?

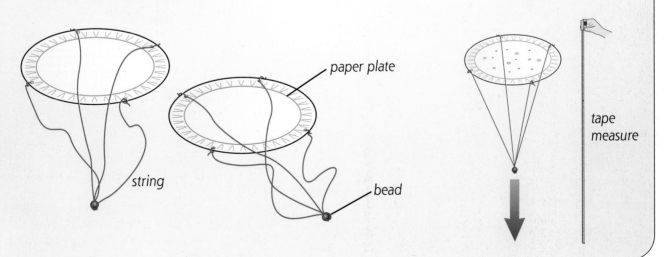

paper plate

string

bead

tape measure

What is water resistance?

Water resistance is another type of friction that slows objects down. It is even stronger than air resistance. Some boats are designed with a streamlined shape to reduce resistance as they travel through the water and through air.

Nature's design

Many sea creatures have streamlined bodies that help them to move easily through the ocean water. Sharks and fish have a slim body, with fins to help them glide and steer. This means they use less energy to swim around. Many boats have been designed with these natural shapes in mind. Speedboats have a pointed front that cuts through the water and air. Sailing boats have a streamlined shape that glides through the water, but wide sails that capture the wind to power them along.

SCIENCE AT WORK

Sharks are one of the fastest swimmers in the ocean. Their smooth, streamlined body cuts through the water, which can be especially useful when hunting. Some sharks can swim at speeds of 69 kilometres (43 miles) per hour – they would overtake the fastest human swimmer!

▼ A shark's streamlined shape makes it a powerful, speedy hunter.

Perfect dive?

Some swimming strokes help to reduce the amount of water resistance when you move through water. During front crawl, for example, your body creates a smooth thin line in the water and your arms cut through the water with very little surface area. Divers try to enter the water with the least surface area, too, so they avoid a splash and a painful bellyflop!

Why do divers point their arms and toes when they enter the water?

▼ **This diver has made a smooth, streamlined shape with his body.**

THE SCIENCE DETECTIVE INVESTIGATES:

Sinking shapes

You will need:
- measuring cylinder • water
- modelling clay • stopwatch

1 Fill the measuring cylinder with water.
2 Use the modelling clay to make some small shapes that would fit inside the cylinder, such as a sphere, a sausage, a flat square or circle, a cube and a cone. Use the same amount of clay for each shape.
3 Hold a shape at the top of the cylinder and drop it into the water. Measure the time it takes to reach the bottom. Record your findings in a table or graph. How does the shape of the clay affect the speed? Do any shapes float on the surface? How will you ensure that your comparisons are fair?

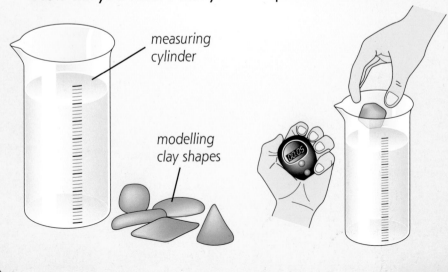

measuring cylinder

modelling clay shapes

Why do some things float and others sink?

The force of gravity pulls on objects in water, in a similar way to its pull on objects in air. This makes some objects sink. The water creates a force in the opposite direction, too. If the weight of an object is equal (or lighter) than the force of the water, the object will float.

Floating

If you try to push a beach ball under water, you will find it very difficult. The beach ball is full of air. Although it is attracted to the ground by the pull of gravity, it is lighter than the water it is trying to push aside. The upward force of the water is greater than the downward force of the ball, so it stays floating. This upward force is called **upthrust**. Air pushes up on objects, too, but because this force is very small we hardly notice it. We can only see this effect if a gas is lighter than air. A helium-filled balloon, for example, is lighter than air, so it 'floats'.

🐾 **Why does a sponge float when it is dry, but sink when it is wet?**

▼ **A beach ball is light and full of air, making it very difficult to push under the water.**

Shape and size

The way that objects float or sink depends on their shape and size, and the material they are made from. Objects that are light for their size, such as a sponge, will float. Objects that are heavy for their size, such as a pebble, will sink. The surface area that touches the water is also important. A large ship carrying **cargo** floats because it is full of air spaces. It is lighter than (or the same weight as) the water it pushes aside. But if the cargo is thrown overboard, the cargo may sink if its surface area is smaller, and it is heavier, than the water it pushes aside.

SCIENCE AT WORK

When submarines travel under water they sink to the seabed and rise to the surface by changing their weight. They have tanks that fill with water or air (to make them heavier or lighter). The air is **compressed** to make it easier to store. When a submarine is heavier than the water it pushes aside, it begins to sink. When it is lighter than the water it pushes aside, it begins to rise.

THE SCIENCE DETECTIVE INVESTIGATES:

Diver in a bottle

You will need:
- modelling clay • paper clip • pen lid with a clip
- 2-litre water bottle • water

1 Make a small diver from the modelling clay. Press a paper clip firmly into the clay 'head' and hang it from the clip of a pen lid.
2 Fill the bottle with water and drop the 'diver' in. The pen lid should float just above the water level. Make your diver bigger or smaller if needed.
3 Screw on the lid of the bottle tightly. Squeeze the bottle for a few seconds and then release. What happens to the diver?

pen lid

paper clip

modelling clay diver

bottle of water

force of gravity pulling the diver

squeeze the bottle

What is pressure?

When you press or push on something, you are adding **pressure**. Blowing up a balloon or pumping up a bicycle tyre, increases the pressure of the air inside. This is because more air is pushing against the same surface area. Pressure increases even more when a force is applied to a smaller area.

Adding pressure

Pressure can be useful for cutting things. A knife and fork increase the pressure of your hand and arm movements when you want to slice and spear your food. The thin prongs of a fork pierce your food, while the knife cuts through it. We also have sharp teeth at the front of our mouths, to help cut and tear our food. A knife can be sharpened to increase its cutting power by wearing the blade into a thin edge. This increases the pressure by reducing the knife's surface area.

▶ **This digger has prongs with a small surface area. They increase the pressure of the digger's force, to cut into the ground.**

SCIENCE AT WORK

There is pressure all around us. The force of gravity pulls air towards the ground, but we don't notice it because pressure in our bodies pushes back at the same time. High above the ground, there is less air pressure. When you fly in an aeroplane, your ears may 'pop' because the pressure of the air inside your ears is greater than the air pressure inside the plane. When your ears pop, it helps to balance the air pressure inside your ears with the air pressure outside.

In a similar way, when you press your finger against a wall, you don't leave a mark, but if you push a drawing pin against the wall, the sharp point leaves a dent or a hole. The sharp point increases the force of your push.

Reducing pressure

A drawing pin also has a flat end. This spreads the force over a greater area, to protect your finger from the sharp point. Today, new cars are fitted with **air bags**. In the event of an accident, the bags inflate. These bags help to spread the force of an impact over a larger area, to keep injuries to a minimum. The bubble wrap we use to package delicate items also helps to reduce pressure. If a parcel is knocked or jolted, the force spreads through the surface of the bubble wrap, reducing the impact and any potential damage.

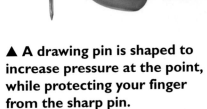

▲ **A drawing pin is shaped to increase pressure at the point, while protecting your finger from the sharp pin.**

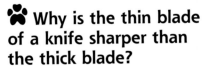

✿ **Why is the thin blade of a knife sharper than the thick blade?**

◄ **When you pack to move house, bubble wrap can help to protect delicate objects by spreading the force of an impact.**

How do we use forces?

We use forces every day to move ourselves and to move the objects around us. Over the years, our knowledge of forces has helped us to create **machines** that produce even greater forces than we can. This makes our work easier.

Forces in nature

Sometimes we use the forces of nature to power things. A boat can be difficult to row across the water, but adding a sail uses the power of the wind to move it along. The boat's streamlined shape glides through the water, while air pushes against the sail to move it faster. Wind **turbines** use the power of moving air, too. As the blades turn, they spin a turbine that turns a **generator** to make electricity. In a **hydroelectric** power station, the force of flowing water works in a similar way, to turn a turbine and generate electricity.

▼ **A wind turbine catches the wind in its blades. When the blades move, they turn a turbine that spins a generator to make electricity.**

SCIENCE AT WORK

Some power stations use the force of moving waves to generate electricity. In a wave power station on the shore, waves wash in and out of a tube of air. This causes the air to move up and down the tube. The force of the moving air turns a turbine that spins a generator to make electricity.

🐾 **Use books or the Internet to find out how a windmill can be used to grind corn or to generate electricity.**

Machines

Our work is made quicker and easier by machines. This is because they make forces bigger or cause forces to change direction. Some machines are simple. A screwdriver, for example, is a simple machine that helps to tighten or loosen screws. As your hand grips the handle and applies a twisting force, the screwdriver increases this force to turn the screw. Other machines are more complicated and need fuel or electricity to work. A car is a complicated machine that uses petrol or diesel to carry passengers along.

▲ **This tractor is powered by fuel. The force of the machine helps to move the bales of hay.**

▶ **Washing machines are powered by electricity. They clean and spin-dry our laundry.**

What are levers and pulleys?

Levers and **pulleys** are simple machines that make lifting easier. Levers are used in many everyday items such as spanners, shoehorns and scissors. Pulleys are found in winches and cranes used on building sites and in industry.

Levers

A lever is a long bar that turns around a fixed point called a **pivot**. To move an object with a lever, a force is applied to one end of the bar, and the object to be moved (the load) is positioned at the other end. Levers make lifting easier by increasing the force that is applied.

If you try to open a paint tin with your fingers, you will find it very difficult. But if you push down on a spoon handle under the lid, it will make it easier. This is because the spoon acts as a lever, pivoting on the edge of the tin. The force of your push at the end of the spoon is multiplied to give a bigger force under the tin lid. By changing the distance between the force, the pivot and the load, you can change the amount of effort needed.

❖ **Why do you think it is easier to lift a paint tin lid with a tablespoon than a teaspoon?**

▼ **A seesaw is a simple lever. When you push on one end of the seesaw, it makes it easier to lift the person on the other side.**

SCIENCE AT WORK

Scissors are an example of a 'double lever'. They have two blades joined together at the pivot. For safety, the blades of craft scissors are not very sharp, but when you squeeze them together, they can cut through paper. If you place the paper close to the pivot, the force of your hand is increased. If the distance from your hand to the pivot is twice the distance of the pivot to the paper, the force will be doubled.

Pulleys

A pulley is another simple machine used for lifting. It can also change the direction of a force. A pulley is a grooved wheel (or set of wheels) with a rope running over it. If you pull down on the rope, it lifts the weight on the other side. If you add more wheels and rope to the pulley, it makes lifting easier. In a similar way to a lever, the additional rope spreads the force over a longer distance.

◀ **A crane uses levers and pulleys to lift and move heavy objects on a building site.**

▼ **In this pulley, a long rope has been divided between a set of wheels. The force needed to lift the weight through this shorter distance is halved.**

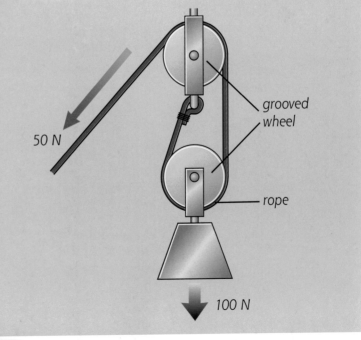

50 N

grooved wheel

rope

100 N

Your project: Forces in action

Forces change the motion of all the objects around us. Our knowledge of forces has helped us to make machines that move efficiently through water and through air. Try this activity to explore how gravity and air resistance affect the movement of a paper glider.

You will need:
• sheets of A4 paper • scissors
• paper clips • tape measure

Method

Your challenge is to make a piece of A4 paper float as far as possible across a room. You can cut and fold the paper to change its shape and you can add paper clips as weights. To make your test fair, however, you must simply release the glider when you let it go, without throwing it into the air.

1   Experiment by making different shapes for your paper glider.

a)   What happens when you screw the paper into a ball and let it go?
b)   What happens when you make it into the shape of an aeroplane?
c)   Can you make your glider more streamlined?
d)   Can you increase the surface area?
e)   Try adding paper clips to make your glider heavier. What effect does this have on the way the glider travels?
f)   Use the tape measure to record the distances that your paper travels, and compare these distances to improve your design.

2   Now try making the example below. Use the illustrations on page 29 as a guide. How does this glider differ to your own designs? Which glider travels the furthest?

a)   Fold and cut the paper to form a right-angled triangle, with two equal sides.
b)   Fold the side opposite the right angle inwards (thinly) two times, and join the ends together to make a hat (like a mitre or Bishop's hat).
c)   Hold your glider horizontally near to the tail (the top of the hat) with the tail on the underside. Release your glider. As it falls, it should gently float across the room.

Explore ways to improve the direction and distance that your glider travels by adding paper clips for weight, changing the centre of balance, and folding the tail up or down.

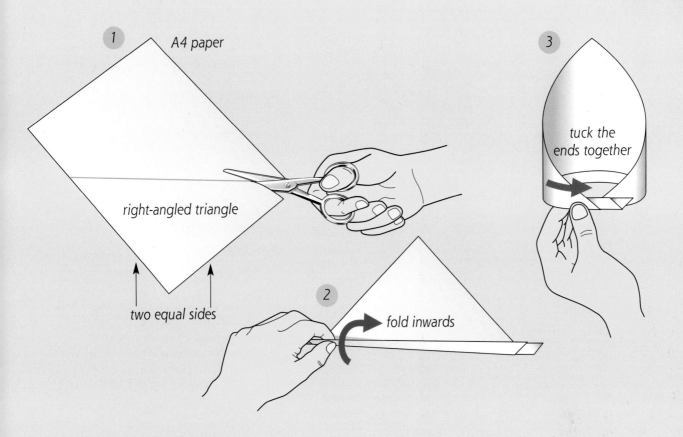

1 A4 paper

right-angled triangle

two equal sides

2 fold inwards

3 tuck the ends together

▼ **This condor has wide wings
to help it soar through the air.**

Glossary

accelerate A measurement of how quickly the speed of a moving object is increasing.

air bag An inflatable rubber bag, often used as a safety device in a car or other vehicle. The air bag inflates upon impact to spread the force of a collision. This prevents passengers injuring themselves in the event of an accident.

air resistance A type of friction affecting objects moving through air.

balanced forces When opposing forces are equal. When forces are balanced an object stays still, or stays moving at the same speed.

blacksmith A person who shapes objects made from iron, by heating them and bending, cutting or flattening them with a hammer.

cargo The goods carried by ships, aircraft or other vehicles, usually to be sold in another location.

compressed To be squashed.

decelerate A measurement of how quickly the speed of a moving object is decreasing.

drag The effect of air resistance.

elasticity When a material is stretched or squashed, but goes back to its original shape and size when the force is removed.

forcemeter A device used to measure the strength of a force in Newtons.

friction A force that slows down the movement of two objects rubbing together. Air resistance and water resistance are types of friction.

generator A machine that uses a magnet to change movement energy into electrical energy.

gravity The invisible force that pulls all materials together across space. The force of gravity on Earth pulls objects towards the Earth's centre. The force of gravity also pulls the Earth towards the Sun's centre.

hydroelectric Electrical energy produced from water power. In a hydroelectric power station, the movement of flowing water spins turbines that turn a generator to create electricity.

impact The force of a collision, when two moving objects come into contact with each other.

lever A simple machine used for lifting weights or for prising something open.

machine A device that helps to make our work easier. Machines can lift, turn or spin objects, for example.

Newton A unit of force. One Newton is the downward force of 100 grams (4 oz).

orbit The curved course of a planet or other body in space. The Earth orbits the Sun, for example.

pivot The point about which a lever turns.

pressure The force that one object exerts on another object when they come into contact.

pulley A simple machine used for lifting weights with a small amount of force. Pulleys are ropes or cables that run around fixed wheels.

resist To oppose movement.

stationary When an object stays still, without movement.

streamlined The design of a body, such as a car, aircraft or ship, that helps it to move smoothly through air or water because it reduces the force of friction.

turbine A machine that can be turned by wind, water or steam. Turbines can be used to spin generators to create electricity.

unbalanced forces When opposing forces are unequal. When forces are unbalanced an object starts moving, changes speed or changes direction.

upthrust The upward force acting on an object, in air or water.

vacuum An empty space that contains no air.

water resistance A type of friction affecting objects moving through water.

weight The measurement of how heavy an object is. Weight is measured in Newtons but we usually convert this to kilogrammes. Weight depends on the force of gravity.

Answers

Page 5: Door (push and pull), doorbell (push), drawer (push and pull), piano key (push), mobile phone (push), sticky tape (pull), shopping trolley (push and pull), snooker cue/balls (push and pull), broom (push and pull), spade (push and pull).

Page 7: Astronauts walk on the Moon in a strange way because their bodies aren't pulled very strongly towards the ground. The force of gravity on the Moon is weaker than on Earth.

Page 7: When the modelling clay is added, the clown stays standing up because the force of gravity pulls the modelling clay towards the ground. If you move the clown, the base stays down and the head flips up.

Page 8: It is difficult to walk on sand because the forces are unbalanced. When the force of your body pushes down on the sand, the sand doesn't push back with an equal force and your feet start to sink.

Page 11: Example answers: elastic band, socks, spring, rubber ball, sponge.

Page 12: To go faster, you need to pedal harder, or cycle down a hill. To slow down, you need to use the brakes or cycle up a hill.

Page 13: The speed of the vehicles changes with the size of the force (release or push), the angle of the slope and the weight of the vehicle. The vehicles go faster when the ramp is steeper (because the force of gravity is increased). The heavier vehicles travel the fastest (because the force of gravity pulls on them the most). The fastest cars tend to travel the furthest. For a fair comparison, the cars and trucks would need to be released (pushed) with the same force, and would need to start at the same point on the ramp. Repeating the test and measurements will help to give a more accurate result.

Page 14: When a car brakes, friction between the rough surface of the tyres and the rough surface of the road helps to slow the car down. When the road is icy, there is less friction and the wheels slide across the smooth surface.

Page 15: It is impossible to pull the telephone directories apart because the force of friction opposes the movement. When you hold one directory up, the other doesn't fall down. When the force of friction covers a big area, it becomes strong. The more pages you overlap, the bigger the area and the greater the force of friction.

Page 17: Sports cars have a smooth, sleek shape to reduce the surface area affected by air resistance. This helps the cars to move faster, with less fuel.

Page 17: The paper plates with the most (or largest) holes travel the fastest, because there is less air resistance preventing their fall. For a fair test, the paper plates would need to be the same size (weight), they would need to be dropped from the same height and released (not thrown), and the lengths of string/weight of the bead would need to be the same. Repeating the test will help to give a more accurate result.

Page 19: Divers point their arms and toes to reduce friction between their body and the water. If water resistance is reduced, they will make less splash.

Page 19: The clay shapes with the least surface area travel the fastest, because there is less water resistance preventing their fall. For a fair test, the shapes would need to be the same size (weight), they would need to be dropped from the same height and released (not thrown), and the same amount of water would need to be in the cylinder. Repeating the test will help to give a more accurate result.

Page 20: A sponge floats when it is dry because it is full of air spaces that make it light for its size. When the sponge is wet, it absorbs the water, becomes heavier and sinks.

Page 21: The diver should sink and then rise again. An air bubble trapped inside the pen lid makes the diver lighter than the water, so it floats. When you squeeze the bottle, water compresses (squashes) this air and the water takes up more space in the pen lid. The diver is now heavier than the water so it sinks. When you release your grip, the air in the pen lid expands again, and the diver rises.

Page 23: The thin blade of a knife is sharper than the thick blade because it has a smaller surface area. When you press on the knife, the pressure on this small area cuts through a surface.

Page 24: A windmill is a machine powered by the force of the wind. The turning blades are connected to a shaft inside the windmill. To grind grain, the turning shaft is connected to two stones that spin and grind the grain between them. To generate electricity, the turning shaft spins a generator to make electricity.

Page 26: It is easier to lift a paint tin lid with a tablespoon because the spoon handle is longer. When the distance between the force and the pivot increases, the force at the other end of the spoon gets bigger.

Websites

http://www.bbc.co.uk/schools/ks2bitesize/science/activies/forces_action.shtml
Learn about forces and try out some fun activities.

http://www.fi.edu/qa97/spotlight3/spotlight3.html
Learn about different types of simple machines.

http://www.physics4kids.com/files/motion_intro.html
Find out more about forces, friction and gravity.

http://www.sciencenewsforkids.org
Keep up with the latest news about forces and motion.

Index